(Im)perfect Blooms

By Erin Clarke

Table of Contents

Depression!

Often we find
stricken minds
are the most adept
at noticing profound
radical beauty,
in the way that
mountain goats' hooves
find purchase on the
tiniest outcroppings
of rock—all but invisible
to our apish eyes—
as they spring
from foothold to foothold
on a sheer cliff face.
Gravity is our teacher,
cruel and stark, heavy and
waiting.
Yet that over-analytical,
relentless introspective gaze
which threatens to pull us
down into free-fall
can too be lasered
on the glory of a snail,
the delicate mesh of baby moss
sweetly cloaking a stone,
and the softness of slippers.
So our doubting brains
clutching at purpose
gather harvests of boundless joy
for the long barren winters,
and those of us who
survive
find ten million things
to live for, and ten million more.

Let me sing you my song
of socks,
it was hard-won.

Forever

"Let's get a tortoise
and have it for 100 years,"
I said,
my naked hand in yours
as our shoulders kissed and held it,
and you chuckled softly
then said, "Okay."
I beamed a ray of light,
delighted–no, alighted–
that you felt it too:
this happiness too big
to fit within the timetable
of our ticking doomsday clocks,
that can and should go on
tending life and living
as it treads along
on tender claws,
slowly chewing greens
and needing things,
while we keep listening,
fingers closing the waxing and waning gap
between us
and love, stubbornly, forever.

(Im)perfect Blooms

Perfection is my addiction
I absorbed through the cord
and the air
and the subtext of each assigned reading
completed early, thank you very much.

Raised to seek blood and trophies,
I stood proudly on the lofty pedestal
with my shaking hands and bouquet of flowers
while I waited, craving
a pat on the head, telling me what a good thing I've been.
Am I good yet? Am I?
No.
Perfection would be better. That's just logic.
The beast has very sensible teeth.

Yet, as I sat in the backyard,
toes in the dirt,
sun stroking the edges of wisping clouds,
I spied a clover flower
among the absolutely perfect A+ specimens
who had a
wonky blotted leaf, a
nick out of the side,
and drooping,
      smushed,
            asymmetrical petals,
that had the
gall
to continue growing anyway;
triumphantly vertical, challenging gravity
and rabbit teeth
and errant boots to dare
to bring it down,

it stood, ugly and absolute,
red-stained and fearless.

It cannot lose.
Its mission is already complete–
it is alive.

The withdrawal shakes stilled

in my aching, weighty limbs.

I vowed from that day
to live
with the audacity of clover.

Smudged, drooping,
panicked and flailing,

I cannot lose.
I am alive.

Be loved

When the body
feels heavy and the heart
drags like soggy clothes,
stairs elongate into infinity
and hauling your limbs
is just too much,
consider the inertia could be
an invitation to come closer–
to enjoy gravity's hug as Earth
holds you, dearly, for safekeeping,

it's a chance to hug her back,
to surrender,

to be held entirely,

the peace of the gigantic
reminding you
you are small
and beloved.

Honor the heavenly bodies.
Lie down.

Blackbird Delight

Nothing beats the view
of a crow from below
a sheet of corrugated vinyl
see-through ceiling,
from the graceless thumped landing
to the jagged strange shadow
above three-pronged stick-figure feet,
to the scratching pounding steps
as it tramps—yes tramps—across
the panel,
and remembering
this cawing
cacophonous creature
can fly wherever it wants,
but chose this place
right above my small self
to scritch-clomp in silly steps
before it rejoins its kin on currents of air,
whose sleek black bodies outnumber mine
15,000 to one.
What a little, lucky one am I.

Mythic

There is one ocean.
It flows and churns ushered and transformed
becoming saltier, brighter, lonelier, deadlier,
before journeying back to be recycled again,
its unknown depths fostering relationships of infinite permutations,
the names and distinctions arbitrary
for our convenience.

There is one ocean.
Our bodies come from it,
these upright mobile contraptions
wired with rivulets of intelligent seawater
rigged to sustain fantastical compilations of cells, beings at play,
consuming and birthing each other, evolving in time.

As the currents and channels
of your blood
nourish your tissues,
I ask you,
Poseidon,
Have you been a merciful god?

Winter Weekend

Cold slow morning dragging
dainty light
filtered through the sluggish, chilled air,
urgency forgotten as the panic-thrum
hibernates–
it is too cold to worry,
it is too light to fear.
We drift as dust motes
dancing in the sunrays,
enjoying the lazy path to landing
nowhere in particular.

Coming Home

Closing the door to leave behind
the thrum and buzz of expected things.

Welcome to the hallowed houses of holy, cavernous headspace,
allowing room for all the things you've forgotten (such as):

You have a body, with a trillion harmonious pieces composing a single,
flowing, supportive whole.

And

Bridges through time connect us all from one heart to another like an
infinite web of unbreakable gossamer threads throughout all human
history (and even before, if you ask the trees.)

And

There is a time before the idea, when quiet inspiration
swims up gently from the depths of silence and takes your breath away.

And

There is a gong vibration that
ripples through your body as stillness settles in,
warm and friendly as a purring cat.

And
You are home.
You always were
You just forgot.

"Welcome back," the pieces whisper lovingly as you see
the entire jigsaw puzzle for
three whole glorious
seconds.

You are home.

Songbird

Perched in our nest, it is your hour,
the space between waking
and the grumbling chores of the day.
You gather your voice and
accompaniments and begin
your call, your song
my songbird,
calling for calling's sake,
the toll of gorgeous vocal bells
a gentle reminder we
are here for the lightness,
for the present moment that
grows—filling our attention
for the length of our surrender,
here for the sweetness of a Friday morning song,
sung to no one,
drifting down to the roses
under the balcony
bobbing in the breeze
out of time.

Keep Going

Because there's nothing else to do.
There is some ticking
machinery, deep in the
metaphysic organs of somewhere
that insists upon it.
With a loving push, it nudges
the tiniest lift
to set you onto the next minute
at least.

This is the place
where you want to weep,
but can't put your finger
on anything worth the
effort of tears,
so you get up and do something:
dishes, painting, battle, or prayer
depending on your upbringing and repression level.

Connecting feet to something
bigger for better or worse,
breathing another moment,
and surrendering to the grand
inertia–the grind of all grinds–
in the hopes that at some point
you get to dance downhill
with ease.

Keep going.
I love you.
Keep going.

No Really, Keep Going

Remember you too are
made of pulsing roots
and wiggle hums
and sluggish rain,
whirling disco ball reflections
and shaking fury.
The sobs and sighs of fog
have nothing on the glory of you.

Power Lines

Mourning dove outposts
and brave squirrel highways,
strung overhead they reach
in joins,
holding hands in coupling connections
of metal on metal
on metal faraway—
it's metal all the way back
to the Ferris wheel
spinning atoms with delight
until their particles whirl
into a new kind of dance.
The edges have to be touching
for the magic to move,
kissing into conductive, delicate mazes,
the electrons circuitously swimming,
wrapping back around
in perfectly balanced harmony
they flow;
all the pieces connected
for miles on end.

The gadgets are love too.

Permission to be a Fuck-up

You are not in the top ten, or the
top ten thousand, you have
no ranking and bumble like
a toddler finding a face-full
of pavement instead of footsteps,
and it's fine.

You seem to not be wired with
the same circuits for success
as others committed to their lucrative
stable careers and enriching
weekend hobbies,
and everyone knows you
won't be buying your own plane
ticket home for Thanksgiving,
and it's fine.

There may not be any
redeeming creative freedom
or madcap whimsical wisdom
that makes up for the differences
between you
and those who give
such an impervious impression
of having their shit together,
and it's fine.

But you cooed with awe
over the perfection of a
banana slug on a rotting tree stump
yesterday, so maybe
cut yourself at least as much slack
as you do living antennaed snot,
dear one.

Quilt

Cut down, stitched together,
enmeshed in mathematics
eyes are courted in lights and darks—
a shape quadrille with
unknown
unnumbered hands
who wrought
this piece for loving warmth;
these bricks mortared with thread
to build a historic embrace...
or I suppose
one could say

it's just a blanket
on a sunny day
after a long, hard journey
that warms the toes
and welcomes you—
stranger—
to this quiet moment alone.

Patience, baby

Sitting in your shining, exhausted virtue,
I invite you to listen to the silence expanding.

The moss will not consume you while you wait.
Your flesh will not give way to the forest yet.

Going against all we know of the outer world,
in here the weeds untangle themselves, shrink down,

the horizon widens, the air freshens,
and the birdsong mutates into an ever-known language,

celebrating your revelations in 5/4 time.
The lies unspool into vapor,

drifting lazily across the sky
with the weight of transitory unimportance.

With patience you are free.

Bugs in the Cauliflower

There are bugs in the cauliflower
I bought, plastic-wrapped and stamped
with the logo of some
vague faraway industrial farm.
I mistook them for a few brown spots on one side
until I undressed the beheaded flower
from its never-degrading sheath
and saw, Oh,
there are so many
dead speckles
of little winged beings
that it looks like a thoroughly peppered
centerpiece;
the remnants of what must have been
a glorious feast for the taking
until they met their end,
their bodies nestled in
nearly every possible crevice
of this fractal forest of white.
There was even a slug, thick
and stagnant under a leaf–
a prize I rarely see outside
my forest wanderings–right here
in my glossy white-cabineted kitchen.

I swell with an odd and secret joy
to be one of so many guests
that have partaken in this
dinner gift, rather than eating alone
with only my kind.

It takes nearly an hour to pick them
all out, the cloth napkin becoming
increasingly cluttered
with constellations of exoskeletons.
I whisper goodbye before
shaking them outside, their bodies
becoming a bird banquet,
and then hum a nondescript gratitude
to be part of this world
at all.

Dear Reader, Read Me Slowly.

Like a nice firm but yielding button that clicks,

like the *kerdunk* of a pen dropped deliberately on a page,

like swishing one's hand through water and watching the wave wrap it
like a glass boxing glove.

Like a well-mixed cup of hot cocoa in a wide-set mug with a thick
handle,

like Gregory Peck's voice,

like book smell.

Like the vibrations from an old wooden pepper grinder,

like finally taking that one bobby pin out which had been jabbing the
scalp all day,

like coming inside from the crisp, clumping snow, and lying in bed,
wrapped in blankets, completely naked.

Like a fresh, perfect sandwich,

like a favorite song ending,

like a smooth pebble foraged from the wild,

we are freed from the
tumbling chorus of wants
one satisfying moment at a time.

Have a Seat (this could be a while)

There is something lurking
in the depths
of my personal black sea,
those familiar brackish waters
cold and unknowable,
until whatever flickering
flitting thing
decides it's time to be glimpsed
at the surface,
like a generous goldfish,
or nightmare turtle,
or a slimy mundane log
that bobbed and weaved
like a magical being
only to remind me the value
of the prosaic.

Something is waiting
to be heard, to be seen,
to be understood.
And until I manage
to shut my brain up
I can never know
if it's a Scottish plesiosaur of legend,
or a single, short-lived bubble.

This is where true listening begins.

In my seat on the bank of the sea
that dies with me,
I wait right back.

Precipitation, Anticipation

Rain seeping into the pores
of the ground,
the wood, the crevices
of boots,
the wetness soaking
all things with squelching
dripping purpose–
it is a gift of
monumental abundance,
this relentless moist
barrage of droplets
from heaven to earth,
and the dirt swells
with possibility,
the creatures harvest and
savor it like fine wine,
the leaves tremble
and spill gargantuan
momentary diamonds
down to adorn their
hidden roots below.

The world is ripe
and ready
when it rains.

I am with you. (Are you with me?)

The longest relationship
you have is with
yourself,
which in many cases means
you've been shacked up
with an abuser ever since
the first moment an adult made you feel small,
imperfect, and selfish
(which, empirically, you probably were.)

The logical fallacies
of your unfinished frontal lobe
owe you better.

I am a survivor too.

Let's hold hands on the count of three.

And if you say we can't...

There are spirits and legacies who have shaped
this Now of ours, such as:

The soul of the tree in this paper,
a being made by a coincidence of dirt
and sun and water, lassoed
by mitochondria and cellulose to make a
living and breathing tower, until it fell,
and was pulped into something new,
bringing fragments of
the forest to your hands.

The person who sketched
their dreams of machines capable
of making books,
those who wrought the steel to build them,
and the foods they ate on their lunch break
as they sat and rested their tired backs,
savoring food harvested and carried, bought
and sold, and cooked and packed with
varying degrees of care by unknown numbers of people.

And long before all of that,

generations of creatures with appendages
growing more and more hand-like
and feet more foot-like
and globular heads with more and more space for dreams
until these beings were called Human,
and more of them had more of them
until one day you arrived in this place,
in this time,
surrounded by these things imprinted
by the histories of trillions of living energies,

So yes, I am with you,
by virtue of these words,
these priceless codes
handed down by generations of
parents and patient public school teachers,
ensuring we could always
have a way into each other's worlds
outside of linear time.

Yes, I am with you now.
Hold hands with me.
One.
Two.
Three.

A Gratitude

The world could have made you all knives,
fingernail filament quills adorning your back
and scales shielding your skin
and venom daggers defining your mouth.
Something was worth
forsaking armor
for snuggles.
For this, I give thanks.

Le Cadre

Bones are crystalline memory;
a partly-living document
perpetually edited by
microbiologic construction monsters
eating and bricklaying every moment
they live according to the blueprints
inside cell goop,
as well as the currents of
pressure-based electricity that
radiate through the strata
with your every move.

These wooden building blocks
that ripple like water
form the framework to which the rest of your
complicated, oddly-shaped, viscous balloons
are tethered.
Your skeleton is a timescape autobiography
written in three-dimensional calcium,
and damn isn't it fascinating to be alive.

Do Nothing

Do nothing like a lion
napping in the shade,
waiting for the heavy sun
to drag across the sky,
for the heat to abate
into cool sweet darkness.

Do nothing like a bird singing
in no particular direction,
taking off in an eye-blink
to another branch
without warning or reason.

Do nothing like a baby hippo
cradled in the river,
doing a slow-motion moon-bounce
as its stamping feet
prance on the rocky bottom.

Do nothing like a rabbit,
back feet splayed out in
relaxation, munching on
a casual dandelion
under the covered comfort
of a blackberry bush.

Do nothing because
it is yours to do, always,
for this earth has fruit and shade
and water and it never
had to be this hard.

Be wild and rest,
It is your birthright.

Swimming

Air is a substrate,
a nourishing background
afterthought.
Its currents, ripples,
and waves are just like
water–only lighter,
faster,
invisible.

Like a slim-tailed fish gulps
water through gills to savor oxygen
as it swims, I drag breath into my lungs
as I dance, shimmying
and swishing in the living room.

What waves are made
by my body, air swelling and rippling as
I swoop to scoop up
my giggling progeny?

What gorgeous fractal
fluid dynamics decorate the
breezes as I run my hand through my hair?

What joy would you feel
glimmering on your perfect skin
if you too realized
you've been swimming
all along?

Human Foibles

A dainty seed—a morsel
of hope and pure potential—
is buried haphazardly among
cold, dead remnants of its
cousins, random space minerals,
and a massive collective of tiny
creatures
stirring and tasting the mix
to get this teeming decomposition mud pie
just right.

In the depths of fecund rotten things
and creeping invertebrates,
damp and absolutely dark,
it manages to sprout.
A single crispy tentacle pushes
its way through and,
without fail,
always goes the right way up
to find a glorious dinner of sun.

We widen our eyes and wonder,
"How does it know where to go?"

Assuming in our meaty wisdom
that "knowing" ever mattered
in the first place.

Conduit

Waves softly loping
across
the mass of softness,
a pond of calm,
the reservoir
from which the ink pours
into letters and words,
spilling gut musings
and heart murmurs
into lyrical beats
for whispering wanting ears,

you are not alone,

you are not alone with
any of it,

everyone made this moment
with desperate hands
in the dark and we
will hum together
as we feel our way
onward
in our vast complex
termite tunnels,
slowly growing
towards the light.

Rest easy, feelings don't scare me

They are a push and a pull,
waves that flow
in give and take,
energy that flits
across as a skipping stone,
leaving its rippling gift
which, once accepted in my
willing hands, dissipates
in frothy nothing,
leaving the next feeling in its wake.

I do not fear my sadness
for I know she will not
drown me, she is my
love for absent things—
the hollowed outline of
my heart singing its wishing songs.

I do not fear my anger
for I know she will not
devour me, she is my knowing
of what's right and just,
rearing her glorious warrior's
head in favor of truth
and kindness.

I do not fear my fear
for I know she will not
hide me forever, her dungeon
walls are not unscalable
and her intentions are good;
she simply expresses her love
in overbearing ways.

And my joy, my beloved
glowing darling who
squeals for inchworms
and sighs at landscapes
and appreciates ice cream
with the fervor it is due,
I have only ever regretted
the moments I tethered her down
and held her back.

Now I could never fear her.
I aim to send her, wild and silly,
to savor every treasure she can find
daily, for as long as we live.
Rest easy.
Feelings do not scare me, and need not scare you.

Softness Song

I was born soft.
We all were—that velvet newborn
head softer than anything, it must
be felt to be believed, just like those
bafflingly sticky brand-new hands
clinging to their grownups' skin
like gecko pads on a sunny wall.

Staying soft is harder—the trick
of unhardening rarely taught,
and a thing re-learned with
each fresh hell;
but only by those dogged
soul-explorers who bother
to follow the nagging whispers
and flickering lights that
lead us down
counterintuitive zig-zag paths
in search of that lasting,
deep, eternal contentment.

Staying soft can feel impossible
as the leaden bricks
of global doom pile on our shoulders
one by one,
the weight compressing
our beings into crushed, despondent,
rageful things,
lashing out at whatever is available
be it barista or boyfriend
or government or self.

But softness is the
only way to survive;
that sweet dropping of the
shoulders, and the exhaled
surrender to the
untamable entropy
of growth. For with softness
we grow too, expanding
with grace wide enough
to enfold agony with
gentleness,
granting us unfathomably

painful and delightful
superpowers
to stand
and feel it
and love regardless.

Be soft, dear warriors,
conquer the density of the times
by dissolving your bones
into clouds
through which the hails
of news-cycle gunfire
pass unscathing.

Rally your grateful
holding heart
to savor
this breath,
a lighthouse beacon
in the tumultuous
sharpening dark,
to be a soft moment
caressed with mutual pleasure
and teach others
what softness
can be.

Be soft and free,
my brave, kind kin,
do not let the burdens hold you.

We can be born and born again
with each remembrance
of how these selves began:
a velvet beloved miracle of chances,
a temporary life in
the symphony of time,
here to add our graceful melodies
in the midst
of grand collective wandering.

Be soft and free,
my brave kind kin,
do not let the burdens hold you.
We have a song to sing.

Acknowledgments

The poem "Depression!" was previously published in Wellspring Humanities and Arts magazine, thank you to the editors.

Thank you to Kristen Kalp, who helped me remember I am a writer, and to Jarod K. Anderson who reminded me of the world's beauty on days I had forgotten.

Thank you to my teachers Melissa Hasebrook, Erin Ergenbright, and Tom Wiseman for their encouragement, kind words, and for giving me literary playgrounds on which to run wild.

Thank you to my parents who always bought me more notebooks.

Thank you, readers, for spending this time with me.

Lastly, I am thankful for Taylor. Thank you, my love, for everything.

Layout and Design by Scott Cannon
Picture Frame Press
Portland, Oregon 2023